My World of Science

SOUND AND HEARING

Angela Royston

Heinemann Library
Chicago, Illinois

Designed by bigtop
Originated by Ambassador Litho
Printed and bound in Hong Kong/China

06 05 04 03 02
10 9 8 7 6 5 4 3 2 1

Library of Congress Cataloging-in-Publication Data

Royston, Angela.
  Sound and hearing.
      p. cm. -- (My world of science)
Includes bibliographical references and index.
  ISBN 1-58810-246-7
1. Sound--Juvenile literature. 2. Hearing--Juvenile literature. [1.
Sound. 2. Hearing.] I. Title.
  QC225.5 .R695 2001
  534--dc21
                              00-012875

Acknowledgments
The author and publishers are grateful to the following for permission to reproduce copyright material:
Mark Burnett/Science Photo Library, p. 14; Trevor Clifford, pp. 7, 15, 16, 17, 19, 21, 23, 24, 27, 29;
G. Daniels, p. 5; Tim Davis, p. 9; Eye Ubiquitous, pp. 8, 10, 28; Robert Harding, p. 22; H. Rogers/Trip,
pp. 4, 6, 11, 20, 25; Stone, pp. 13, 18, 26; Jonathan Watts, p. 12.

Cover photograph reproduced with permission of Trevor Clifford.

Every effort has been made to contact copyright holders of any material reproduced in this book.
Any omissions will be rectified in subsequent printings if notice is given to the publisher.

Some words are shown in bold, like this. You can find out what they mean by looking in the glossary.

Contents

What Is Sound?

Sound is what we hear when something makes a noise. This dog is barking. People near it can hear the sounds it makes.

Sometimes you can hear many noises at the same time. The people in this street can hear many sounds, such as the sound of cars and people talking.

Making Sounds

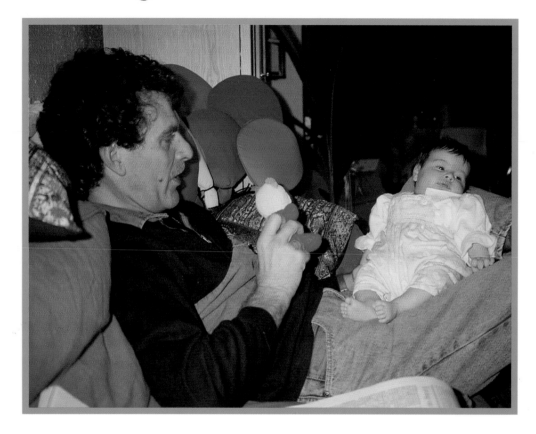

There are many different ways to make sounds. This father is shaking a rattle to make a noise. Banging, scraping, and rubbing also make sounds.

These children are making plenty of
loud noise. Each child is making sounds
in a different way.

Describing Sounds

There are many words to describe how a noise sounds. These bells make a "ding-dong" sound. An alarm clock makes a different kind of ringing noise.

Spanish dancers sometimes use **castanets.** The dancer makes a clicking sound with the castanets. She makes a stomping sound with her feet.

Loud and Quiet

If you bang something hard, it will make a loud noise. If you just tap it, it will make a soft noise.

This cat is purring quietly because it is happy. If the cat is hungry, hurt, or upset it will make a loud meow sound.

Vibrations in the Air

When you **pluck** the string of a guitar, it moves back and forth very fast. This makes the air around it **vibrate.**

The vibrating air makes the sound.
The **vibrations** move through the air
like the ripples move on a pond.

Ears and Hearing

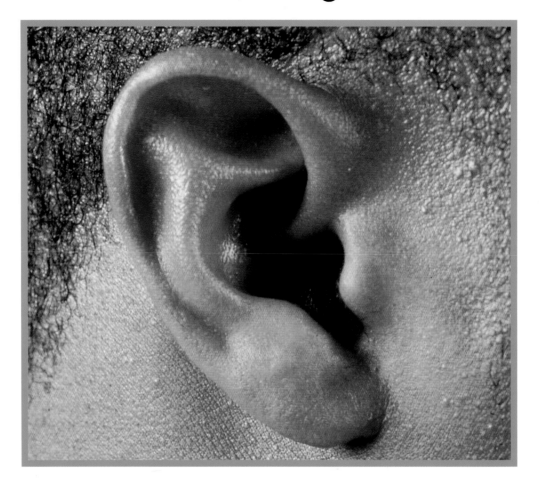

You hear sounds when **vibrations** in the air reach your ears. The vibrating air makes your **eardrum vibrate.** The vibrations pass inside your ear.

If you cover your ears with your hands or with **earmuffs,** you cannot hear as well. This is because less moving air reaches your eardrums.

Talking

People can make sounds and talk because we have **vocal cords** in our throats. As you breathe out, the air makes the cords **vibrate.**

Put your hand on your throat and make a noise. You will feel the cords vibrating. You make different sounds by moving your lips and tongue.

Musical Sounds

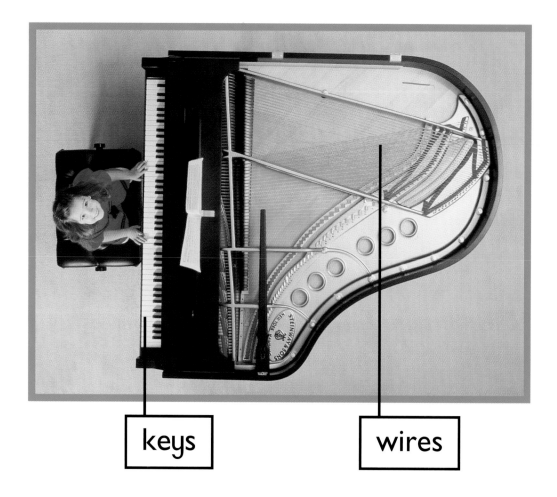

keys

wires

Instruments make air **vibrate** in different ways. Piano keys are joined to hammers inside the piano. When you press a key, a hammer hits a wire and makes it vibrate.

When you blow into a recorder or a trumpet, you make the air inside it vibrate. When you bang a drum, the top vibrates.

High and Low

Musical instruments make many different notes. A thin violin string makes a high note. A thick string makes a low note.

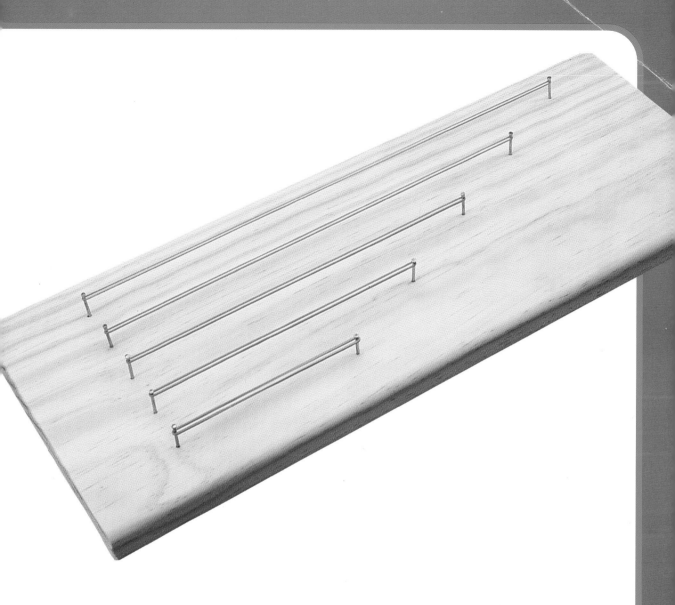

You can make an instrument by stretching rubber bands between nails. The rubber band stretched tightest will make the highest note.

Sound Travels

Sounds are louder the closer you are to them. The noise of this airplane becomes quieter and fainter as the plane flies farther away.

Put your ear next to a glass of soda. You will hear the bubbles bursting. When you move away from the glass, the sounds no longer reach you.

Hearing but Not Seeing

Sound can travel around corners.
The boy can hear the sound the two
girls are making. He cannot see who
is making the sound.

Sound can travel through wood, water, and most other things. The people in the house cannot see who is knocking on the door, but they can hear the sound.

Where Is It Coming From?

Sometimes it is hard to tell where a sound is coming from. When you cross the road, you must look as well as listen for traffic.

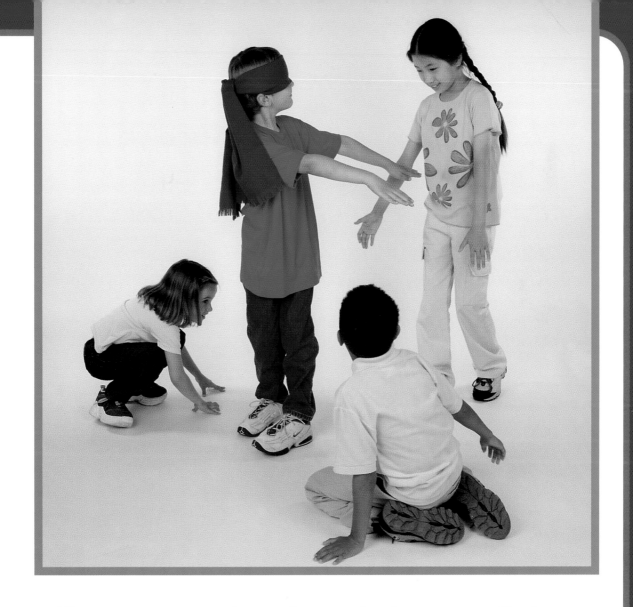

Turning your head can help you tell the direction of a sound. When you cannot see, you must listen hard for any noises.

Dangerous Sound

Very loud noises can **damage** your ears. These men are wearing ear covers to **protect** their ears from the sound of drilling.

If you listen to music through headphones, make sure the sound is not too loud. Take care of your hearing so that you can hear for many years.

Glossary

castanets instrument made of two pieces of wood that are clicked together by the fingers

damage hurt or injure

eardrum very thin sheet of skin in your ear

earmuffs things you put over your ears to keep them warm

pluck to pull strings with the fingers

protect to keep safe

vibrate to move a small distance back and forth very fast

vibrations very fast movements backward and forward

vocal cords pieces of skin that vibrate when you speak, making noise

More Books to Read

Burton, Margie, Cathy French, and Tammy Jones. *Sounds.* Pelham, N.Y.: Benchmark Education Co., 1998.

Hewitt, Sally. *Hearing Sounds.* Danbury, Conn.: Children's Press, 1998.

Pfeffer, Wendy. *Sounds All Around.* New York: HarperCollins Children's Book Group, 1999.

Index